This notebook is _____ tion, which are inspire _____ ngel Wings made a significant impact in my life or that of someone I love.

When I asked my cousin what her mom's favorite color was, she wasn't sure if she had one, but she knew that she loved yellow roses. I started with the yellow background (my second favorite color), then added the roses, the flares, and the bling. This beauty then spoke to me and screamed "I Got Sunshine"! Ms. Gwendolyn is up in heaven reunited with her daughter and other loved ones, praising God for no more rain.

I pray that this stunning notebook cover and it's equally beautiful inspirational color pages bring a smile and warm feelings to your heart, especially on cloudy days.

This Burst of Sunshine Notebook, Belongs To:

_____

"If you spend your whole life waiting for the storm, you'll never see the Sunshine".   Morris West

Date:_____/_____/_____

Notes, Ideas, Dreams, Visions

"Arise, shine for your light has come, And the glory of the Lord has risen upon you. Isaiah 60:1 (NIV)

Date:_____/_____/_____

Notes, Ideas, Dreams, Visions

"Arise, shine for your light has come, And the glory of the Lord has risen upon you. Isaiah 60:1 (NIV)

Date:_____/_____/_____

Notes, Ideas, Dreams, Visions

"Arise, shine for your light has come, And the glory of the Lord has risen upon you. Isaiah 60:1 (NIV)

Date:_____/_____/_____

Notes, Ideas, Dreams, Visions

"Arise, shine for your light has come, And the glory of the Lord has risen upon you. Isaiah 60:1 (NIV)

Date:_____/_____/_____

Notes, Ideas, Dreams, Visions

"Arise, shine for your light has come, And the glory of the Lord has risen upon you. Isaiah 60:1 (NIV)

Date:_____/_____/_____
Notes, Ideas, Dreams, Visions

"Arise, shine for your light has come, And the glory of the Lord has risen upon you. Isaiah 60:1 (NIV)

Date:_____/_____/_____

Notes, Ideas, Dreams, Visions

"Arise, shine for your light has come, And the glory of the Lord has risen upon you. Isaiah 60:1 (NIV)

Date:_____/_____/_____
Notes, Ideas, Dreams, Visions

"Arise, shine for your light has come, And the glory of the Lord has risen upon you. Isaiah 60:1 (NIV)

Date:_____/_____/_____
Notes, Ideas, Dreams, Visions

"Arise, shine for your light has come, And the glory of the Lord has risen upon you. Isaiah 60:1 (NIV)

Date:_____/_____/_____
Notes, Ideas, Dreams, Visions

"Arise, shine for your light has come, And the glory of the Lord has risen upon you. Isaiah 60:1 (NIV)

Date:_____/_____/_____
Notes, Ideas, Dreams, Visions

"Arise, shine for your light has come, And the glory of the Lord has risen upon you. Isaiah 60:1 (NIV)

Date:_____/_____/_____
Notes, Ideas, Dreams, Visions

"Arise, shine for your light has come, And the glory of the Lord has risen upon you. Isaiah 60:1 (NIV)

Date:_____/_____/_____
Notes, Ideas, Dreams, Visions

"Arise, shine for your light has come, And the glory of the Lord has risen upon you. Isaiah 60:1 (NIV)

Date:_____/_____/_____
Notes, Ideas, Dreams, Visions

"Arise, shine for your light has come, And the glory of the Lord has risen upon you. Isaiah 60:1 (NIV)

Date:_____/_____/_____

Notes, Ideas, Dreams, Visions

_____
_____
_____
_____
_____
_____
_____
_____
_____
_____
_____
_____
_____
_____
_____
_____
_____
_____
_____
_____
_____
_____
_____
_____
_____
_____

"Arise, shine for your light has come, And the glory of the Lord has risen upon you. Isaiah 60:1 (NIV)

Date:_____/_____/_____

Notes, Ideas, Dreams, Visions

_____
_____
_____
_____
_____
_____
_____
_____
_____
_____
_____
_____
_____
_____
_____
_____
_____
_____
_____
_____
_____
_____
_____
_____

"Arise, shine for your light has come, And the glory of the Lord has risen upon you. Isaiah 60:1 (NIV)

Date:_____/_____/_____
Notes, Ideas, Dreams, Visions

"Arise, shine for your light has come, And the glory of the Lord has risen upon you. Isaiah 60:1 (NIV)

Date:_____/_____/_____
Notes, Ideas, Dreams, Visions

"Arise, shine for your light has come, And the glory of the Lord has risen upon you. Isaiah 60:1 (NIV)

Date: _____ / _____ / _____

Notes, Ideas, Dreams, Visions

"Arise, shine for your light has come, And the glory of the Lord has risen upon you. Isaiah 60:1 (NIV)

Date:_____/_____/_____

Notes, Ideas, Dreams, Visions

_____
_____
_____
_____
_____
_____
_____
_____
_____
_____
_____
_____
_____
_____
_____
_____
_____
_____
_____
_____
_____
_____
_____
_____
_____
_____

"Arise, shine for your light has come, And the glory of the Lord has risen upon you. Isaiah 60:1 (NIV)

Date:_____/_____/_____

Notes, Ideas, Dreams, Visions

"Arise, shine for your light has come, And the glory of the Lord has risen upon you. Isaiah 60:1 (NIV)

Date:_____/_____/_____
Notes, Ideas, Dreams, Visions

"Arise, shine for your light has come, And the glory of the Lord has risen upon you. Isaiah 60:1 (NIV)

Date:_____/_____/_____

Notes, Ideas, Dreams, Visions

"Arise, shine for your light has come, And the glory of the Lord has risen upon you. Isaiah 60:1 (NIV)

Date:_____/_____/_____

Notes, Ideas, Dreams, Visions

_____
_____
_____
_____
_____
_____
_____
_____
_____
_____
_____
_____
_____
_____
_____
_____
_____
_____
_____
_____
_____
_____
_____
_____

"Arise, shine for your light has come, And the glory of the Lord has risen upon you. Isaiah 60:1 (NIV)

Date: _____ / _____ / _____

Notes, Ideas, Dreams, Visions

"Arise, shine for your light has come, And the glory of the Lord has risen upon you. Isaiah 60:1 (NIV)

Date:_____/_____/_____
Notes, Ideas, Dreams, Visions

"Arise, shine for your light has come, And the glory of the Lord has risen upon you. Isaiah 60:1 (NIV)

Date:_____/_____/_____

Notes, Ideas, Dreams, Visions

"Arise, shine for your light has come, And the glory of the Lord has risen upon you. Isaiah 60:1 (NIV)

Date:_____/_____/_____

Notes, Ideas, Dreams, Visions

_____
_____
_____
_____
_____
_____
_____
_____
_____
_____
_____
_____
_____
_____
_____
_____
_____
_____
_____
_____
_____
_____
_____
_____
_____
_____

"Arise, shine for your light has come, And the glory of the Lord has risen upon you. Isaiah 60:1 (NIV)

Date:_____/_____/_____
Notes, Ideas, Dreams, Visions

"Arise, shine for your light has come, And the glory of the Lord has risen upon you. Isaiah 60:1 (NIV)

Date:_____/_____/_____

Notes, Ideas, Dreams, Visions

"Arise, shine for your light has come, And the glory of the Lord has risen upon you. Isaiah 60:1 (NIV)

Date:_____/_____/_____
Notes, Ideas, Dreams, Visions

"Arise, shine for your light has come, And the glory of the Lord has risen upon you. Isaiah 60:1 (NIV)

Date:_____/_____/_____

Notes, Ideas, Dreams, Visions

_____
_____
_____
_____
_____
_____
_____
_____
_____
_____
_____
_____
_____
_____
_____
_____
_____
_____
_____
_____
_____
_____
_____
_____
_____
_____
_____
_____

"Arise, shine for your light has come, And the glory of the Lord has risen upon you. Isaiah 60:1 (NIV)

Date:_____/_____/_____
Notes, Ideas, Dreams, Visions

"Arise, shine for your light has come, And the glory of the Lord has risen upon you. Isaiah 60:1 (NIV)

Date:_____/_____/_____
Notes, Ideas, Dreams, Visions

"Arise, shine for your light has come, And the glory of the Lord has risen upon you. Isaiah 60:1 (NIV)

Date:_____/_____/_____
Notes, Ideas, Dreams, Visions

"Arise, shine for your light has come, And the glory of the Lord has risen upon you. Isaiah 60:1 (NIV)

Date:_____/_____/_____
Notes, Ideas, Dreams, Visions

"Arise, shine for your light has come, And the glory of the Lord has risen upon you. Isaiah 60:1 (NIV)

Date:_____/_____/_____

Notes, Ideas, Dreams, Visions

"Arise, shine for your light has come, And the glory of the Lord has risen upon you. Isaiah 60:1 (NIV)

Date:_____/_____/_____
Notes, Ideas, Dreams, Visions

"Arise, shine for your light has come, And the glory of the Lord has risen upon you. Isaiah 60:1 (NIV)

Date:_____/_____/_____

Notes, Ideas, Dreams, Visions

"Arise, shine for your light has come, And the glory of the Lord has risen upon you. Isaiah 60:1 (NIV)

Date:_____/_____/_____
Notes, Ideas, Dreams, Visions

"Arise, shine for your light has come, And the glory of the Lord has risen upon you. Isaiah 60:1 (NIV)

Date:_____/_____/_____

Notes, Ideas, Dreams, Visions

"Arise, shine for your light has come, And the glory of the Lord has risen upon you. Isaiah 60:1 (NIV)

Date:_____/_____/_____

Notes, Ideas, Dreams, Visions

"Arise, shine for your light has come, And the glory of the Lord has risen upon you. Isaiah 60:1 (NIV)

Date:_____/_____/_____
Notes, Ideas, Dreams, Visions

"Arise, shine for your light has come, And the glory of the Lord has risen upon you. Isaiah 60:1 (NIV)

Date:_____/_____/_____

Notes, Ideas, Dreams, Visions

_____
_____
_____
_____
_____
_____
_____
_____
_____
_____
_____
_____
_____
_____
_____
_____
_____
_____
_____
_____
_____
_____
_____
_____
_____
_____
_____
_____

"Arise, shine for your light has come, And the glory of the Lord has risen upon you. Isaiah 60:1 (NIV)

Date:_____/_____/_____

Notes, Ideas, Dreams, Visions

"Arise, shine for your light has come, And the glory of the Lord has risen upon you. Isaiah 60:1 (NIV)

Date:_____/_____/_____

Notes, Ideas, Dreams, Visions

"Arise, shine for your light has come, And the glory of the Lord has risen upon you. Isaiah 60:1 (NIV)

Date:_____/_____/_____

Notes, Ideas, Dreams, Visions

"Arise, shine for your light has come, And the glory of the Lord has risen upon you. Isaiah 60:1 (NIV)

Date:_____/_____/_____
Notes, Ideas, Dreams, Visions

"Arise, shine for your light has come, And the glory of the Lord has risen upon you. Isaiah 60:1 (NIV)

Date:_____/_____/_____

Notes, Ideas, Dreams, Visions

"Arise, shine for your light has come, And the glory of the Lord has risen upon you. Isaiah 60:1 (NIV)

Date:_____/_____/_____

Notes, Ideas, Dreams, Visions

_____
_____
_____
_____
_____
_____
_____
_____
_____
_____
_____
_____
_____
_____
_____
_____
_____
_____
_____
_____
_____
_____
_____
_____
_____
_____
_____
_____
_____
_____

"Arise, shine for your light has come, And the glory of the Lord has risen upon you. Isaiah 60:1 (NIV)

Date:_____/_____/_____

Notes, Ideas, Dreams, Visions

"Arise, shine for your light has come, And the glory of the Lord has risen upon you. Isaiah 60:1 (NIV)

Date:_____/_____/_____
Notes, Ideas, Dreams, Visions

"Arise, shine for your light has come, And the glory of the Lord has risen upon you. Isaiah 60:1 (NIV)

Date:_____/_____/_____
Notes, Ideas, Dreams, Visions

"Arise, shine for your light has come, And the glory of the Lord has risen upon you. Isaiah 60:1 (NIV)

Date:_____/_____/_____

Notes, Ideas, Dreams, Visions

"Arise, shine for your light has come, And the glory of the Lord has risen upon you. Isaiah 60:1 (NIV)

Date:_____/_____/_____
Notes, Ideas, Dreams, Visions

"Arise, shine for your light has come, And the glory of the Lord has risen upon you. Isaiah 60:1 (NIV)

Date:_____/_____/_____

Notes, Ideas, Dreams, Visions

"Arise, shine for your light has come, And the glory of the Lord has risen upon you. Isaiah 60:1 (NIV)

Date:_____/_____/_____

Notes, Ideas, Dreams, Visions

"Arise, shine for your light has come, And the glory of the Lord has risen upon you. Isaiah 60:1 (NIV)

Date:_____/_____/_____

Notes, Ideas, Dreams, Visions

"Arise, shine for your light has come, And the glory of the Lord has risen upon you. Isaiah 60:1 (NIV)

Date:_____/_____/_____

Notes, Ideas, Dreams, Visions

"Arise, shine for your light has come, And the glory of the Lord has risen upon you. Isaiah 60:1 (NIV)

Date:_____/_____/_____

Notes, Ideas, Dreams, Visions

"Arise, shine for your light has come, And the glory of the Lord has risen upon you. Isaiah 60:1 (NIV)

Date:_____/_____/_____

Notes, Ideas, Dreams, Visions

_____
_____
_____
_____
_____
_____
_____
_____
_____
_____
_____
_____
_____
_____
_____
_____
_____
_____
_____
_____
_____
_____
_____
_____
_____
_____
_____

"Arise, shine for your light has come, And the glory of the Lord has risen upon you. Isaiah 60:1 (NIV)

Date:_____/_____/_____
Notes, Ideas, Dreams, Visions

"Arise, shine for your light has come, And the glory of the Lord has risen upon you. Isaiah 60:1 (NIV)

Date:_____/_____/_____

Notes, Ideas, Dreams, Visions

"Arise, shine for your light has come, And the glory of the Lord has risen upon you. Isaiah 60:1 (NIV)

Date:_____/_____/_____
Notes, Ideas, Dreams, Visions

"Arise, shine for your light has come, And the glory of the Lord has risen upon you. Isaiah 60:1 (NIV)

Date:_____/_____/_____

Notes, Ideas, Dreams, Visions

"Arise, shine for your light has come, And the glory of the Lord has risen upon you. Isaiah 60:1 (NIV)

Date:_____/_____/_____
Notes, Ideas, Dreams, Visions

"Arise, shine for your light has come, And the glory of the Lord has risen upon you. Isaiah 60:1 (NIV)

Date:_____/_____/_____

Notes, Ideas, Dreams, Visions

_____
_____
_____
_____
_____
_____
_____
_____
_____
_____
_____
_____
_____
_____
_____
_____
_____
_____
_____
_____
_____
_____
_____
_____
_____

"Arise, shine for your light has come, And the glory of the Lord has risen upon you. Isaiah 60:1 (NIV)

Date:_____/_____/_____

Notes, Ideas, Dreams, Visions

"Arise, shine for your light has come, And the glory of the Lord has risen upon you. Isaiah 60:1 (NIV)

Date:_____/_____/_____
Notes, Ideas, Dreams, Visions

"Arise, shine for your light has come, And the glory of the Lord has risen upon you. Isaiah 60:1 (NIV)

Date:_____/_____/_____
Notes, Ideas, Dreams, Visions

"Arise, shine for your light has come, And the glory of the Lord has risen upon you. Isaiah 60:1 (NIV)

Date:_____/_____/_____

Notes, Ideas, Dreams, Visions

"Arise, shine for your light has come, And the glory of the Lord has risen upon you. Isaiah 60:1 (NIV)

Date:_____/_____/_____

Notes, Ideas, Dreams, Visions

"Arise, shine for your light has come, And the glory of the Lord has risen upon you. Isaiah 60:1 (NIV)

Date:_____/_____/_____
Notes, Ideas, Dreams, Visions

"Arise, shine for your light has come, And the glory of the Lord has risen upon you. Isaiah 60:1 (NIV)

Date:_____/_____/_____
Notes, Ideas, Dreams, Visions

"Arise, shine for your light has come, And the glory of the Lord has risen upon you. Isaiah 60:1 (NIV)

Date:_____/_____/_____

Notes, Ideas, Dreams, Visions

"Arise, shine for your light has come, And the glory of the Lord has risen upon you. Isaiah 60:1 (NIV)

Date:_____/_____/_____
Notes, Ideas, Dreams, Visions

"Arise, shine for your light has come, And the glory of the Lord has risen upon you. Isaiah 60:1 (NIV)

Date:_____/_____/_____
Notes, Ideas, Dreams, Visions

"Arise, shine for your light has come, And the glory of the Lord has risen upon you. Isaiah 60:1 (NIV)

Date:_____/_____/_____
Notes, Ideas, Dreams, Visions

"Arise, shine for your light has come, And the glory of the Lord has risen upon you. Isaiah 60:1 (NIV)

Date:_____/_____/_____

Notes, Ideas, Dreams, Visions

"Arise, shine for your light has come, And the glory of the Lord has risen upon you. Isaiah 60:1 (NIV)

Date:_____/_____/_____
Notes, Ideas, Dreams, Visions

"Arise, shine for your light has come, And the glory of the Lord has risen upon you. Isaiah 60:1 (NIV)

Date:_____/_____/_____

Notes, Ideas, Dreams, Visions

"Arise, shine for your light has come, And the glory of the Lord has risen upon you. Isaiah 60:1 (NIV)

Date:_____/_____/_____

Notes, Ideas, Dreams, Visions

_____
_____
_____
_____
_____
_____
_____
_____
_____
_____
_____
_____
_____
_____
_____
_____
_____
_____
_____
_____
_____
_____
_____
_____
_____
_____

"Arise, shine for your light has come, And the glory of the Lord has risen upon you. Isaiah 60:1 (NIV)

Date:_____/_____/_____

Notes, Ideas, Dreams, Visions

_____
_____
_____
_____
_____
_____
_____
_____
_____
_____
_____
_____
_____
_____
_____
_____
_____
_____
_____
_____
_____
_____
_____
_____
_____
_____
_____
_____

"Arise, shine for your light has come, And the glory of the Lord has risen upon you. Isaiah 60:1 (NIV)

Date:_____/_____/_____
Notes, Ideas, Dreams, Visions

"Arise, shine for your light has come, And the glory of the Lord has risen upon you. Isaiah 60:1 (NIV)

Date:_____/_____/_____

Notes, Ideas, Dreams, Visions

"Arise, shine for your light has come, And the glory of the Lord has risen upon you. Isaiah 60:1 (NIV)

Date:_____/_____/_____
Notes, Ideas, Dreams, Visions

"Arise, shine for your light has come, And the glory of the Lord has risen upon you. Isaiah 60:1 (NIV)

Date:_____/_____/_____

Notes, Ideas, Dreams, Visions

_____
_____
_____
_____
_____
_____
_____
_____
_____
_____
_____
_____
_____
_____
_____
_____
_____
_____
_____
_____
_____
_____
_____
_____
_____
_____

"Arise, shine for your light has come, And the glory of the Lord has risen upon you. Isaiah 60:1 (NIV)

Date:_____/_____/_____

Notes, Ideas, Dreams, Visions

_____
_____
_____
_____
_____
_____
_____
_____
_____
_____
_____
_____
_____
_____
_____
_____
_____
_____
_____
_____
_____
_____
_____
_____
_____
_____

"Arise, shine for your light has come, And the glory of the Lord has risen upon you. Isaiah 60:1 (NIV)

Date:_____/_____/_____

Notes, Ideas, Dreams, Visions

"Arise, shine for your light has come, And the glory of the Lord has risen upon you. Isaiah 60:1 (NIV)

Date:____/____/____

Notes, Ideas, Dreams, Visions

"Arise, shine for your light has come, And the glory of the Lord has risen upon you. Isaiah 60:1 (NIV)

Date:_____/_____/_____
Notes, Ideas, Dreams, Visions

"Arise, shine for your light has come, And the glory of the Lord has risen upon you. Isaiah 60:1 (NIV)

Date:_____/_____/_____

Notes, Ideas, Dreams, Visions

"Arise, shine for your light has come, And the glory of the Lord has risen upon you. Isaiah 60:1 (NIV)

Date:_____/_____/_____

Notes, Ideas, Dreams, Visions

"Arise, shine for your light has come, And the glory of the Lord has risen upon you. Isaiah 60:1 (NIV)

Date:_____/_____/_____

Notes, Ideas, Dreams, Visions

"Arise, shine for your light has come, And the glory of the Lord has risen upon you. Isaiah 60:1 (NIV)

Date: _____ / _____ / _____

Notes, Ideas, Dreams, Visions

_____
_____
_____
_____
_____
_____
_____
_____
_____
_____
_____
_____
_____
_____
_____
_____
_____
_____
_____
_____
_____
_____
_____
_____
_____

"Arise, shine for your light has come, And the glory of the Lord has risen upon you. Isaiah 60:1 (NIV)

Date:_____/_____/_____

Notes, Ideas, Dreams, Visions

"Arise, shine for your light has come, And the glory of the Lord has risen upon you. Isaiah 60:1 (NIV)

Date:_____/_____/_____

Notes, Ideas, Dreams, Visions

"Arise, shine for your light has come, And the glory of the Lord has risen upon you. Isaiah 60:1 (NIV)

Date:_____/_____/_____

Notes, Ideas, Dreams, Visions

"Arise, shine for your light has come, And the glory of the Lord has risen upon you. Isaiah 60:1 (NIV)

Date: _____/_____/_____

Notes, Ideas, Dreams, Visions

_____
_____
_____
_____
_____
_____
_____
_____
_____
_____
_____
_____
_____
_____
_____
_____
_____
_____
_____
_____
_____
_____
_____
_____
_____
_____
_____

"Arise, shine for your light has come, And the glory of the Lord has risen upon you. Isaiah 60:1 (NIV)

Date:_____/_____/_____

Notes, Ideas, Dreams, Visions

"Arise, shine for your light has come, And the glory of the Lord has risen upon you. Isaiah 60:1 (NIV)

Date:_____/_____/_____

Notes, Ideas, Dreams, Visions

"Arise, shine for your light has come, And the glory of the Lord has risen upon you. Isaiah 60:1 (NIV)

Date:_____/_____/_____

Notes, Ideas, Dreams, Visions

"Arise, shine for your light has come, And the glory of the Lord has risen upon you. Isaiah 60:1 (NIV)

Date:_____/_____/_____
Notes, Ideas, Dreams, Visions

"Arise, shine for your light has come, And the glory of the Lord has risen upon you. Isaiah 60:1 (NIV)

Date:_____/_____/_____
Notes, Ideas, Dreams, Visions

"Arise, shine for your light has come, And the glory of the Lord has risen upon you. Isaiah 60:1 (NIV)

Date:_____/_____/_____

Notes, Ideas, Dreams, Visions

"Arise, shine for your light has come, And the glory of the Lord has risen upon you. Isaiah 60:1 (NIV)

Date:_____/_____/_____

Notes, Ideas, Dreams, Visions

"Arise, shine for your light has come, And the glory of the Lord has risen upon you. Isaiah 60:1 (NIV)

Date:_____/_____/_____
Notes, Ideas, Dreams, Visions

"Arise, shine for your light has come, And the glory of the Lord has risen upon you. Isaiah 60:1 (NIV)

Date:_____/_____/_____

Notes, Ideas, Dreams, Visions

_____
_____
_____
_____
_____
_____
_____
_____
_____
_____
_____
_____
_____
_____
_____
_____
_____
_____
_____
_____
_____
_____
_____
_____
_____
_____
_____

"Arise, shine for your light has come, And the glory of the Lord has risen upon you. Isaiah 60:1 (NIV)

Date:_____/_____/_____

Notes, Ideas, Dreams, Visions

"Arise, shine for your light has come, And the glory of the Lord has risen upon you. Isaiah 60:1 (NIV)

Date:_____/_____/_____

Notes, Ideas, Dreams, Visions

"Arise, shine for your light has come, And the glory of the Lord has risen upon you. Isaiah 60:1 (NIV)

Date:_____/_____/_____

Notes, Ideas, Dreams, Visions

"Arise, shine for your light has come, And the glory of the Lord has risen upon you. Isaiah 60:1 (NIV)

Date:_____/_____/_____

Notes, Ideas, Dreams, Visions

"Arise, shine for your light has come, And the glory of the Lord has risen upon you. Isaiah 60:1 (NIV)

Date:_____/_____/_____

Notes, Ideas, Dreams, Visions

_____
_____
_____
_____
_____
_____
_____
_____
_____
_____
_____
_____
_____
_____
_____
_____
_____
_____
_____
_____
_____
_____
_____
_____
_____
_____

"Arise, shine for your light has come, And the glory of the Lord has risen upon you. Isaiah 60:1 (NIV)

Date:_____/_____/_____
Notes, Ideas, Dreams, Visions

"Arise, shine for your light has come, And the glory of the Lord has risen upon you. Isaiah 60:1 (NIV)

Date:_____/_____/_____

Notes, Ideas, Dreams, Visions

"Arise, shine for your light has come, And the glory of the Lord has risen upon you. Isaiah 60:1 (NIV)

Date:_____/_____/_____

Notes, Ideas, Dreams, Visions

"Arise, shine for your light has come, And the glory of the Lord has risen upon you. Isaiah 60:1 (NIV)

Date:_____/_____/_____

Notes, Ideas, Dreams, Visions

_____
_____
_____
_____
_____
_____
_____
_____
_____
_____
_____
_____
_____
_____
_____
_____
_____
_____
_____
_____
_____
_____
_____
_____
_____

"Arise, shine for your light has come, And the glory of the Lord has risen upon you. Isaiah 60:1 (NIV)

Date:_____/_____/_____

Notes, Ideas, Dreams, Visions

"Arise, shine for your light has come, And the glory of the Lord has risen upon you. Isaiah 60:1 (NIV)

Cynthiasauthorplace.com

Copyright © 2021 By Cynthia Chatman Lumsey, Extraordinary Faith

All rights reserved. No part of this publication may be reproduced, distributed, or transmitted in any form or by any means without the prior written consent of the author, except in the case of brief annotations and quotations embodied in reviews and certain other non-commercial uses permitted by the U.S. Copyright.

Scripture quotations marked **NKJV** and **NIV** are taken from the Bible New King James Version and New International Version.

Made in the USA
Columbia, SC
23 August 2022